MY MAGICAL GROUP ROSTER

NAME	EMAIL	PHONE

I0086507

MY INITIAL MAGICAL GROUP NOTES

(some thoughts I'm bringing to the gatherings)

⌘

THE MOST MAGICAL SECRET

A 6-Session Action Guide for Magical Groups and Individuals

SCOTT GROSSBERG

⌘

ANCIENT MAGIC PUBLISHING

ALSO BY SCOTT GROSSBERG

The Most Magical Secret - 4 Weeks to an Ecstatic Life

The Vitruvian Square -
A Handbook of Divination Discoveries

The Deck of Shadows

The Masks of Tarot

THE MOST
MAGICAL SECRET
A 6-Session Action Guide for Magical Groups and Individuals

scottgrossberg.com

THE MOST MAGICAL SECRET: A 6-Session Action Guide for Magical Groups and Individuals. Copyright © 2015 by Scott Grossberg. All rights reserved. No part of this publication may be reproduced, distributed, or transmitted in any form or by any means without the prior written permission of the publisher or author, except in the case of brief quotations embodied in reviews and certain other noncommercial uses permitted by copyright law.

The advice and strategies contained herein may not be suitable for your individual situation. It is sold with the understanding that neither the author nor publisher are engaged in rendering legal, financial, medical, or other professional services. If you require such assistance, you should seek the advice of a competent professional. The author and publisher assume no responsibility for any errors or omissions. The author and publisher expressly disclaim any responsibility for any liability, loss or risk, personal or otherwise, or loss of profit or other commercial damages which might be incurred as a consequence, directly or indirectly, of the use and application of any of the contents of this book, and the techniques, tips, and recommendations suggested or provided.

Before using any of the techniques in *The Most Magical Secret - 4 Weeks to an Ecstatic Life* or this Action Guide, in general, and the walking and breathing methods that are explained, in particular, please make sure you check with your doctor or other health care professional. The suggestions in this book are not meant to replace medical advice and should only be used as a supplement to your normal health care if you are given permission to do so by your health care professional. Neither the author nor the publisher can take any responsibility for any adverse effects from the techniques, methods, and tips offered. When you are not sure of any aspect of what is described in this book, or you feel unwell, seek proper medical advice.

Publisher: Ancient Magic Publishing

ISBN: 978-0-692-53679-7

1. Personal Success 2. Self Help 3. Mind and Body 4. New Age

First Edition

Published in the United States of America.

For more information, send email to:

sgrossberg@hotmail.com

or write to:

Scott Grossberg
8038 Haven Ave.
Suite E
Rancho Cucamonga, CA 91730

The brief quotes and sayings in this book are provided to benefit the public, to illustrate and clarify the author's observations and in furtherance of the author's teaching, scholarly work, education, research, and commentary, and offered through "fair use" as that term is used by the U.S. Copyright Office. All respective names, trademarks, quotes, slogans, and logos mentioned in this book remain the property of their respective owners. The use of any trademarks in this book does not vest in the author or publisher any trademark ownership rights in such trademarks, nor does the use of such trademarks imply any affiliation or endorsement of this book by such owners. Any brand names or individual names are used in an editorial fashion.

GROUP OPENING

I am Magic.

I stir the Universe and in turn become its purpose.

I am a companion of the legends. The fables. The fanciful.

I am a way.
A direction.
A path worth taking.

The secret door that leads to a real life.

I show others how to be an ally of myth
and find the truth in fantasy.

I teach others that their intentions are as strong as steel
and their realms are as extraordinary as any miracle.

I help others hear the whispered voice of hope,
feel the hidden presence of desire,
and see the invisible impulse of passion.

I am the stolen moments when power is reclaimed.

I am a hunger for,
a pull to,
an expectation of what really matters.

I don't pretend anymore.

I am Magic.

GROUP CLOSING

I can.

I will.

I dare.

I am.

I am The Power.

I am The Magic.

I can accomplish the impossible.

I will completely devour life.

I dare to be passionately curious.

I do whatever it takes.

I am invincible.

Take my heart and set it on fire that

I may give it to the world.

PERSONAL MANTRA/AFFIRMATION

Real Magic is about making choices.

I choose a life of

Passion

Confidence

Daring

Plenty

My Happily Ever After starts now.

ADDITIONAL MANTRAS/AFFIRMATIONS

(some slogans I have discovered that empower me)

⌘

CONTENTS

A SPECIAL MAGICAL NOTE   1
FOR ACTION GROUP LEADERS

ONE MORE MAGICAL NOTE   8
FOR SOLITARY ADVENTURERS

"SAYING AND DOING" WITH YOUR ACTION GUIDE   13

A SOURCE OF IMAGINATION AND PERHAPS A LITTLE MORE
GUIDANCE FOR YOUR MAGICAL GROUP   19
MY BEST ADVICE FOR ACTION GROUP LEADERS

SESSION ONE   24
I WILL CREATE MAGIC IN THE WORLD

SESSION TWO   31
I WILL REGAIN MY POWER

SESSION THREE   38
I WILL STOP PRETENDING AND GET ON WITH LIVING

SESSION FOUR   45
I WILL FIND A WAY FORWARD AND FOLLOW IT

SESSION FIVE   52
I WILL OPEN THE SECRET DOOR TO A REAL LIFE

SESSION SIX   60
I WILL LIVE A LIFE THAT TRULY MATTERS

FREQUENTLY ASKED QUESTIONS   67

MY ACTION GROUP PLEDGE   71

WHERE TO FIND OTHER MAGICIANS   73

YOUR MAGICAL GROUP CALENDAR   76

ANSWER KEY   77

A NOTE ON THE AUTHOR   80

A SPECIAL MAGICAL NOTE
For Action Group Leaders

If your actions inspire others to dream more,
learn more, do more and become more,
you are a leader.
                                        - John Quincy Adams

[NOTE: If you are not planning on leading an Action Group and, instead, are going to work through this Action Guide on your own, please skip ahead to the next chapter.]

This Action Guide was created to help you lead and facilitate a small magical group gathering to further deepen and embed the techniques from *The Most Magical Secret - 4 Weeks to an Ecstatic Life*. Organizing and conducting such an Action Group is both simple and a lot of fun!

Gather Your Small Group of Magicians

Before you ask even one person to join you in the study and practice of *The Most Magical Secret*, you need to determine what you personally want to accomplish with the group. You're going to find that the combination of wonder, excitement, and power of any small group of Magicians is incredible. You're also going to discover that you are able to appreciate and manifest more with such a group than if you simply study alone. That's not to take anything away from the solo practitioners out there (I've certainly done my fair share of learning on my own). But, the connection you will make with your group is undeniable and there's a separate kind of Magic in such a gathering of enchanting souls.

That means, of course, that you need to begin by asking yourself the question: "Who would I want to share my dreams and aspirations and ambitions with?" We all have acquaintances we're comfortable around but they're not really the ones we care to become transparent with. Find the people who, when you look into their eyes and when they say your name, make you feel like you've arrived home. Whether you select participants in a calculated or impromptu fashion, make certain that they understand the specific purpose for their attendance. You want people who will demonstrate a serious dedication to their preparation for and participation in what is to come.

Don't be surprised, by the way, when—much like you'll learn about your Object of Affection—your magical attendees FIND YOU.

The next consideration is a practical one: Are you going to create an Action Group with people who physically meet or a gathering that meets virtually (for example, using Google Hangouts or Skype) or simply by phone)? My experience is that assembling a group of people who meet face-to-face is a more effective and manageable approach.

When you are ready to send out your invitations, here is an email template that you are free to use or adapt to your special circumstances. Remember, this isn't a sales letter. It's an request to participate in something special from a family member or a friend.

EMAIL SUBJECT LINE: A Magical Invitation

BODY OF THE EMAIL:

You're Invited to Join an Exclusive Group

Dear [fill in your family member's or friend's name] -

I'm so excited to share a new discovery with you. It's a book called, "The Most Magical Secret - 4 Weeks to an Ecstatic Life." It's all about creating a life of abundance. I thought it would be fun to share what I'm learning with you. So, I've decided to put together a Magical Action Group built around the teachings from the book and its companion Action Guide.

I want to keep this selective and unique (it's going to be a very small group of friends and family). I only want people to share in this who are passionate about finding their purpose in life and making their dreams come true. I'm positive this will be one of the most powerful, fun, and intense experiences you'll ever have.

We're going to help each other create magical lives.

But . . . this is a 6-session, once-a-week commitment! Each session will be about 1 ½ - 2 hours. You'll also need to have a copy of the book and the companion Action Guide.

If you're interested in joining me on an amazing adventure, here's what you can do:

1. Ask yourself if you would like to create something more than you have right now.

2. Ask yourself if you're willing to invest 6 sessions, once-a-week, in order to be happier and more successful at home and at work.

3. Respond back to this email letting me know that you'd like to join me.

4. Wait for my return email letting you know the dates for our Action Group meetings.

5. When you join our Action Group, bring an open mind, your curiosity, your enthusiasm, and get ready to make incredible new discoveries about yourself and your passions.

I'm sending you this, now, because I don't want you to miss out on this remarkable gathering.

Let me know, by replying to this email if you're interested. I'm working on the 6 meeting dates and location now.

Of course, if you have any questions, let me know.

[End with your name]

Encourage the Magic

Your small group of Magicians is going to benefit from your leadership and organization and passion. The following sessions are all designed to bring you the maximum return for the time allotted. As such, I strongly recommend that you create a meeting schedule ahead of time for each of the 6 sessions. (There's a Magical Group Calendar form you can use at the back of this guide.)

You don't want to gather your group only to find out that there are calendar conflicts and then you have to address the loss of momentum that such a challenge creates. Once you have your own scheduling worked out, you can then invite others to participate. You might have to tweak one or two of the meetings a bit. But, you must remain cognizant of and committed to how each of the 6 sessions ties in with the 4-week schedule outlined in *The Most Magical Secret*.

Your group is also going to profit from the accountability that each attendee brings to the others. Each individual's Magic is sparked, grows, and brings about results when they share with each other. It is your job to encourage a fellowship whereby each attendee feels that they are being heard and getting the most out of the gathering.

By the way, when a group of friends and captivating souls get together, it's so very easy for the meeting to turn into a discussion of just about everything in the world. One of your tasks as the leader of the group is to keep everyone centered on the task at hand—creating and experiencing an ecstatic life.

Let the Magic Breathe

This Action Guide is designed to steer you through a course that will bring you wonder, joy, and incredible results. But, it is not supposed to be a taskmaster (nor should you become one as the leader of the group).

Let the outline and direction provided in these pages inspire you, transport you, and keep pushing you. Let yourself and the others respond to what's provided here. At the same time, be open to spontaneous revelations and ideas and needs that will inevitably pop up at every meeting. If you're too rigid with scheduling and time allotments, you will miss some amazing opportunities to help each other grow.

Magic lives in the Present. That means everyone needs to feel free to express themselves at each gathering in a way that furthers their own intentions. You want to leave each session feeling completed.

A Brief Discussion of Timing

One of the logistical elements you will need to decide is when to use this Action Guide in relation to an individual working his or her way through *The Most Magical Secret*. I recommend that you organize your gathering and work through the sessions a week in advance of the items that the book asks a person to do. For example, Session One would take place the week before Day 1 of Magic is undertaken because it covers the preparatory activity that needs to take place. Session Two would take place right before the Day 1 activity. Session Three would take place right before the Day 8 activity and so on.

In the book, when I set forth the 4 Weeks of Magic, I urge people not to work through the days ahead of time. However, it's perfectly acceptable, in the context of your Action Group, to take the days in blocks of 7 at a time because of the different type and extra attention that is being given through the use of this guide.

The sessions are intended to last 1 ½ - 2 hours. If people want to show up a ½ hour early and talk about other things, that's fine. Just make sure that you allow yourself the 1 ½ - 2 hours to focus on the Action Guide. You've been given more information in this Action Guide than you can easily work through in that time frame. You don't want to use up valuable time having light and informal small talk.

Take the time to review the individual session materials and pick and choose the quotations and other discussion points you want to cover. Some will be more important to you than others. Some will just seem to speak to the dynamics of your Action Group. Members can always go back and consider what wasn't covered in the group setting.

When you choose to use the fill-in-the-blanks material, the idea is for you, as the session leader, to provide the answers and then discuss what those answers mean.

And In The Beginning You Must Create

One last thing before we move on. Being an Action Group leader is not something you improvise and it is certainly not something I recommend performing based on your hunches. This Action Guide, for example, is not a simple retelling nor a shorter reproduction of *The Most Magical Secret*. Rather, this Action Guide is filled with brand new content that has its roots in the book but which is designed to take you even deeper into some concepts in a more profound and thoughtful way.

I encourage you, then, to consider the following strategy for turning your Action Group into something extraordinary.

ACTION GROUP LEADER CHECKLIST

EACH WEEK BEFORE YOUR GROUP MEETS

☐ Use the Initial Group Notes page at the beginning of this Action Guide to put into specific words what you want to achieve with your Action Group.

☐ Actually work through the pages from *The Most Magical Secret* that apply to the session you are about to lead.

☐ Keep a journal of thoughts, impressions, new ideas, and sudden understanding that you would like to make certain that the Action Group talks about.

☐ Review the two Action Group mantras/affirmations at the beginning of this Action Guide so that you are completely familiar with the lines and what they mean to you. You don't have to memorize them. Still, they should flow easily from you so that the group can say the words with you and draw from your confidence.

BEFORE EACH GROUP SESSION

☐ Look over the Action Guide material for the session you're about to lead. There are 6 Sessions; each one designed to cover one week's worth of material.

☐ Study the quotes that are provided in each session. These quotes are there for a reason. Take the time to meditate upon each of them and write out what they say to you on a personal level so that you can, in turn, lead a discussion with your Action Group and elicit their responses to the sayings.

☐ Study the Answer Key in the back of the Action Guide for the session you are about to lead. You will be providing the answers to your group members and then leading them through a discussion of those answers.

☐ Take some time for yourself. This Action Guide is as much for you as anyone else. Make certain that you feel empowered and passionate and devoted to the material. You are on a sacred journey to self-awareness, success, and happiness. This isn't only about serving the needs of the Action Group.

ONE MORE MAGICAL NOTE
For Solitary Adventurers

The whole course of human history may
depend on a change of heart
in one solitary and even humble individual –
for it is in the solitary mind and soul of the individual
that the battle between good and evil
is waged and ultimately won or lost.
- M. Scott Peck

[NOTE: If you have already read the preceding chapter and are planning on leading an Action Group, please skip ahead to the next chapter.]

You will see that I mention small groups a lot in this Action Guide. That's not to take away from you if you decide to use this handbook as a way to privately supplement your study and experience of *The Most Magical Secret*. You can easily use all of the methods, suggestions, and information in these pages, as well. You will simply be taking on the roles of both leader and attendee.

Gather Both Your Attention and Intention

Before you begin to explore or choose to revisit *The Most Magical Secret*, you need to determine what you personally want to accomplish through your personal study. Are you willing to give your devout attention and commit your whole intention to creating a life of Magic? If you can do so, as with the suggested group study, I personally know that you're going to find that the combination of wonder, excitement, and power you encounter will be incredible.

Here are some questions to consider in choosing a solitary journey through *The Most Magical Secret*:

1. Why do I want to live a life of Magic?

2. Why do I want to choose a solitary path of magical study rather than sharing my adventure with others of a like mind?

3. Am I willing to eventually share what I learn and discover about my personal Magic?

4. Am I willing to make the world a better place through my magical study?

By the way, don't be stunned if, as you make your way through the book for the first time or again, you suddenly determine that you want to include others in your pilgrimage. If you make such a discovery, just go back and read the preceding chapter and start applying the group concepts.

Encourage Your Personal Magic

Some of the best benefits of your self-study of *The Most Magical Secret* are that you get to choose the right amount of analysis and contemplation for the particular topics you find important. You also have complete control over the time that you spend on your practice and examination of the topics covered by this Action Guide and the book.

The other thing you will gain from your solitary study is that you can spend the time needed to listen to and appraise the self-talk that will take place.

Remember to take the time to clear an adequate space to start and carry through with your new adventure. This should include making certain that you won't be disturbed during the time you allot to this Action Guide and the book. Turn off your cell phone. Turn off your landline.

Turn off the television. Turn off your computer. Let those who might be around know that you need some alone time. You get the point.

You will want to develop a way to hold yourself accountable for completing the Action Guide exercises and moving through the book. Some of you are already excellent at making a resolution and then making it happen. If you're not one of those people, consider posting your intentions online periodically (you can always join us and post online at *The Most Magical Secret* private Facebook group and get accountability that way) or find someone who, although they aren't working through all this with you, will be a cheerleader for you and keep you on task.

Let Your Personal Magic Breathe

You are going to be solely in charge of your pacing as you make your way through this Action Guide. Let this outline and the direction provided inspire you, transport you, and let yourself continue to be pushed. Let yourself respond to what's provided here. At the same time, be open to spontaneous revelations and ideas and needs that will inevitably come to you through every session.

Another Brief Discussion of Timing

You will need to decide when to use this Action Guide in relation to working your way through *The Most Magical Secret*. I recommend that you make your way through the Action Guide sessions a week in advance of the items that the book asks you to do. For example, you would study Session One of this Action Guide the week before the book's Day 1 of Magic is undertaken because it covers the preparatory activity that needs to take place. Session Two would then take place right before the actual Day 1 activity. Session Three would take place right before the Day 8 activity and so on.

In the book, when I set forth the 4 Weeks of Magic, I urge people not to work through the days ahead of time. However, it's perfectly acceptable, in the context of using this Action Guide, to take a look through the days in blocks of 7 at a time because of the different type and extra attention that is being given through the use of this Action Guide.

And In The Beginning You Must Create

One last thing before we move on. This Action Guide is not a simple retelling nor a shorter reproduction of *The Most Magical Secret*. Rather, this Action Guide is filled with brand new content that has its roots in the book but which is designed to take you even deeper into some concepts in a more profound and thoughtful way.

I encourage you, then, to consider the following strategy for turning your personal study of the book into something extraordinary.

SOLITARY STUDY CHECKLIST

EACH WEEK BEFORE YOU BEGIN YOUR STUDY

☐ Use the Initial Group Notes page at the beginning of this Action Guide to put into specific words what you want to achieve with your solitary study.

☐ Actually work through the pages from *The Most Magical Secret* that apply to the particular session you are about to study and work through.

☐ Keep a journal of thoughts, impressions, new ideas, and sudden understanding that come to you. You will want to revisit these writings and discover even deeper meaning the second (or third or fourth) time around.

☐ Review the two Action Group mantras/affirmations at the beginning of this Action Guide. You will be using them, as well. You want to be completely familiar with the lines and what they mean to you. You don't have to memorize them. Even though you are a solitary practitioner, you will want to say them out loud at the beginning and end of your session and let the words develop a life of their own.

BEFORE EACH SOLITARY STUDY SESSION

☐ Look over the Action Guide material for the session you're about to study. There are 6 Sessions; each one is designed to cover one week's worth of material.

☐ Study the quotes that are provided in each session. These quotes are there for a reason. Take the time to meditate upon each of them and write out what they say to you on a personal level.

☐ Study the Answer Key in the back of the Action Guide for the session you are about to study. You will be filling in the answers on your own.

☐ Make certain that you feel empowered and passionate and devoted to the material contained in *The Most Magical Secret* and this Action Guide. You are on a sacred journey to self-awareness, success, and happiness.

"SAYING AND DOING" WITH YOUR ACTION GUIDE

Start by doing what's necessary;
then do what's possible;
and suddenly you are doing the impossible.
- Francis of Assisi

Congratulations! You've made the choice to live a magical life. This Action Guide has been created to help you start and complete a 6-session program based on *The Most Magical Secret* that will nourish, bolster, and enhance that decision.

Here are some thoughts to consider as you begin your adventure:

Magical Group Dynamics

The idea behind your group is to bring your collective wisdom, intentions, and ambitions together to form something truly powerful. Your gathering is also about encouraging each other and holding each of you accountable for your action steps. Your group of Magicians will bring about massive change for each other. To help build the necessary fellowship, at the beginning of each action session, you might want to repeat the following in unison:

I am Magic.

I stir the Universe and in turn become its purpose.

I am a companion of the legends. The fables. The fanciful.

I am a way. A direction. A path worth taking.

The secret door that leads to a real life.

I show others how to be an ally of myth and find the truth in fantasy.

I teach others that their intentions are as strong as steel and their realms are as extraordinary as any miracle.

I help others hear the whispered voice of hope, feel the hidden presence of desire, and see the invisible impulse of passion.

I am the stolen moments when power is reclaimed.

I am a hunger for, a pull to, an expectation of what really matters.

I don't pretend anymore.

I am Magic.

The Backdrop For Each Session

There are 6 sessions included with this Guide; 1 for each of the 4 weeks of Magic from the book and 2 additional gatherings. Each session is self-contained and there are places in the Action Guide for group members to "fill-in-the-blanks" as each meeting progresses. The Answer Key for the "fill-in-the-blanks" sections is in the back of this Guide. The session leader should use these answers to keep the group on track and to spark discussion.

Magical Questions and Action Items

Your Action Guide is designed to help members work their way through each week's lessons and goals. This isn't a race and members are not in competition to see who can finish first. Rather, the included questions and topics are carefully designed to foster collaboration, fellowship, and some deep thinking about what your members want to achieve week-to-week. That being said, you don't want things to drag on. Keep an even pace and an undefended heart as you work through each session.

Journal Pages

Each session comes with two journal pages; one for you to create notes about your dreams, action items, and desired results, and the other for you to take notes about your fellow Magicians. Write down thoughts, ideas, and a "to-do" list as they come to you during each meeting. You won't be able to remember everything. By keeping handwritten notes, you free yourself to become fully engaged in each discussion rather than worrying about what you might forget.

Closing the Meeting

In ending your meeting, I recommend the Action Group use the following:

I can.

I will.

I dare.

I am.

I am The Power.

I am The Magic.

I can accomplish the impossible.

I will completely devour life.

I dare to be passionately curious.

I do whatever it takes.

I am invincible.

Take my heart and set it on fire that I may give it to the world.

Individual Work

As you work your way through *The Most Magical Secret* and this Action Guide, use the following mantra/affirmation to keep you focused, energized, and moving forward:

Real Magic is about making choices.

I choose a life of

Passion

Confidence

Daring

Plenty

My Happily Ever After starts now.

To make this mantra/affirmation even more effective, say the words out loud.

When you're ready to explore this in even more fascinating, wonderful, and exciting ways, repeat the mantra/affirmation over and over again as you meditate upon each and every word and what each word means in the context of what is being said. For example, you would repeat the mantra/affirmation putting emphasis on the word "real" and reflecting upon just that word while the balance of the mantra/affirmation is said. Then you repeat the mantra/affirmation again with emphasis on the word "magic." You continue to breakdown the mantra/affirmation over and over until you get to the last word—"now."

Naturally, you can use the foregoing technique in conjunction with the Walking Meditation described in *The Most Magical Secret*.

Finally, keep in mind that the Action Group and your Action Group leader are there to support you, encourage you, and keep you accountable. However, they are not babysitters. They are not going to do your magical work for you. Nor should they want to. Take ownership of your destiny and the dreams that are about to come true. Earnestly study *The Most Magical Secret* content and then apply those principles to the sessions in this Action Guide.

Here's a checklist to help you get the most out of your meetings:

ACTION GROUP MEMBER CHECKLIST

EACH WEEK BEFORE YOUR GROUP MEETS

☐ Use the Initial Group Notes page at the beginning of this Action Guide to put into specific words what you want to achieve by being a member of your Action Group.

☐ Actually work through all the pages from *The Most Magical Secret* that apply to the session you are about to attend.

☐ Commit to attending each session and sharing yourself, your dreams, and your accomplishments with others.

BEFORE EACH GROUP SESSION

☐ Take some time to privately compose yourself and gather your thoughts before you meet with the group. You are on a sacred journey to self-awareness, success, and happiness.

☐ Commit to being of service to the Action Group leader and your fellow members. There are places in this Action Guide that will allow you to capture your thoughts, impressions, ideas, and suggestions for the others.

AFTER EACH GROUP SESSION

☐ Immediately after each group session, write down your impressions of what has happened during your meeting. These notations should include specific actions that you have promised you will do, outcomes you have claimed you will manifest, and new habits you have pledged to adopt.

A SOURCE OF IMAGINATION AND PERHAPS A LITTLE MORE GUIDANCE FOR YOUR MAGICAL GROUP

MY BEST ADVICE
FOR ACTION GROUP LEADERS
(because I've been right where you are)

I saw the angel in the marble
and carved until I set him free.
- Michelangelo

I want you to take pride in your decision to put together such an incredible cast of characters. I don't know if you're meeting in your own home, in your office, in someone else's home or office, or in a restaurant. The locale doesn't mater as much as making certain that you're able to carry out your own expectations and meet your own needs as well as the group's. There's a reason you chose to take on the role of a leader. Be honest with yourself as to what you want that role to look like long before you ever assemble your group. If you aren't honest with yourself at this early stage, the group dynamics can take over your overall objectives and soon, if you're not careful, you will begin to feel beholden to the group and dissatisfied. Neither of those feelings is conducive to finding and growing your own Magic.

While I want you to determine your own needs and wants for the group, I also want you to breathe a little easier by understanding that this is a powerful group you're piecing together. Once you start this group—once you put out the call for people to join with you—there's a vitality that develops that is more than any one of you could muster on your own.

Here are some additional thoughts for you:

1. **You want to facilitate and manage, not dictate or babysit.** One of the simplest ways to ensure smooth sailing is to form this group with a co-founder. Perhaps there's that "one" person you just know would bring a special spark and charm to the group. Talk to that person candidly about what you have in mind and see if they'd like to take this journey with you. It can be trying at times. You are not collecting a group of ordinary beings. You are gathering people who, if they're not already powerful, will be. These are people whose confidence will be climbing. These are like-minded souls who will be bursting with excitement and want to share with you and the others. You can imagine, then, how all this energy will need to be channeled. Having a co-founder helps. Whether you use a co-founder or not, keep in mind that it is the quality of the group—not the size—that matters most. You want people who will participate and contribute, not just watch and take.

2. **Be open and be authentic.** First of all, others are not likely to join your magical group if they don't believe they can trust you and if the group doesn't have something to offer them in the first place. Even Magicians—perhaps Magicians most of all—ask the question, "What's in it for me?" While you will be going through changes with everyone else as the group moves through the exercises, some things won't change: your trustworthiness, your

reliability, and your leadership. Forming this group is filling a gap you need filled in your own life. Just admit it and honor it.

3. **Don't Ad-Lib Your Meetings.** People are joining your group and coming to your meetings for any number of reasons. They want a better way to learn to live a life of Magic. They want companionship and fellowship during their adventure. They want encouragement, confirmation, and maybe even some prodding. They want to be held accountable. They want a safe place to both succeed and fail. It is your responsibility to know, ahead of time, what you want to accomplish and cover each session. If you don't prepare in advance, then you run the risk of the entire meeting turning in a direction that is neither positive nor productive. You can always veer from the suggested course from time to time. If you prepare for a particular session by reading through this Action Guide before the initial meeting and then glancing through it again before each session, you can make informed decisions as the meeting progresses.

4. **Each person's Magic is individual, unique, and makes itself known at varied times and in different ways.** Okay, you already knew this. Why am I repeating it? Because the stuff you are going to be covering and practicing and doing is electrifying. Because you are going to get impatient at one point or another. Because others are going to get restless at one point or another. I'm reminding you so you can remind others that this isn't a race. There's no prize for the fastest Magician. There are only results. And results show up for each of us at the appropriate time. My results aren't going to behave according to your schedule. No one else's outcomes will either. You are not here to judge anyone's Magic. You are here to encourage and assist and channel the group energy.

That being said, you might discover, after the group is formed, that someone is not participating or not really fitting in in a way that becomes disruptive, uncomfortable, or difficult. I recommend taking this person aside, privately, and explaining the situation as you see it. You can then ask them, "If you were me, what would you do?" More times than not, the person already has an inkling that this isn't the right time for them to be part of the group. Let people who come to this realization take their leave with grace and dignity.

5. **Use this Action Guide as-is. You can improve upon it later.** I get it. You're a Magician. You're creative. You're a self-starter. You're filled to the brim with imagination and you love to take things and make them your own. Take a breath. I've created this Action Guide with particular goals in mind and covering topics in a definite order. I certainly don't mind you making whatever course corrections need to happen for your particular group. Still, there are session objectives that I encourage you to follow for the maximum and most thrilling results.

6. **Be willing to connect with group members outside of group sessions.** Each group session will be filled with lots and lots of discussion. In fact, I have found you will have quite a challenge, at times, in just getting the group session focused on this Action Guide since your new family of Magicians is going to want to have catch-up time at the beginning of each get-together. The end of each formal session will also be filled with members just wanting to share more or take what was discussed to an even deeper level than was possible during the time you provided. Encourage each member to reach out to the others and provide whatever additional support and encouragement might be needed. You can use the phone, email, and social media to great effect.

7. **Commitment, sharing, privacy, and attendance are crucial.** Nothing will derail your Action Group faster than members who aren't committed to living a life of Magic. Nothing will weaken your group dynamics faster than someone who isn't willing to participate (for whatever reason). Nothing will undermine a member's Magic more effectively than a feeling that what they say won't remain private, inviolate, and exclusive to the group unless and until they say otherwise. And nothing will weaken your Action Group faster than members treating their presence at sessions as optional. In selecting your members, make certain that they understand the obligation of being part of this inner group. It's only 6 sessions. If they can't commit to, share during, keep

things confidential, and attend for 6 weeks, they just aren't the right fit.

If you do find that a member has to legitimately miss one of the sessions (I'll leave that determination to your discretion), you might consider recording the gathering. Please don't record anything without the entire group's agreement to do so. If a member does miss a meeting, I also recommend that the absent member agree to connect personally and privately with each of the other members so they can catch up with each other before the next session.

8. **You don't have to guide the group for all 6 sessions.** In fact, if you'd like to mix things up a bit, I recommend that you rotate leaders for the opening and closing mantras. You can also alternate different people to start off a discussion of each of the Days of Magic. I do recommend, however, that you be in charge of wrangling the group together at the start of each session and then graciously ending each gathering.

9. **A little more leadership inspiration for you.** As you put your group together and before each of the sessions, take a look at the following quotes. Consider each of them as a special Magic all their own. I have chosen these with great care for you. They have served me well. I know they will do the same for you.

Lead me, follow me, or get out of my way.
- George S. Patton, Jr.

A leader is best when people barely know he exists, when his work is done, his aim fulfilled, they will say: we did it ourselves.
- Lao Tzu

Where there is no vision, the people perish.
- Proverbs 29:18

Whatever you are, be a good one.
- Abraham Lincoln

SESSION ONE
I WILL CREATE MAGIC IN THE WORLD

Planning For Your Days of Magic

- Go around the room and get to know each other. Now would be a great time to review the Action Group Pledge starting on page 14.

- How do you describe Magic?

Necessary Magic

> *Being busy does not always mean real work.*
> *The object of all work is production or accomplishment*
> *and to either of these ends there must be*
> *forethought, system, planning, intelligence,*
> *and honest purpose, as well as perspiration.*
> *Seeming to do is not doing.*
> — Thomas A. Edison

As a group, start working through Session One. It is designed to coincide with pages 78-97 of *The Most Magical Secret*. The session leader should use the Answer Key on page 77 to help guide the meeting. When a quote appears, use that to examine how it applies to your choice to be a Magician and your desired outcomes. Take lots of notes in this Action Guide. Then, have a spirited group discussion and refer back to both your notes and this Action Guide to keep all of you focused and moving forward.

> *Life's most persistent and urgent question is,*
> *"What are you doing for others?"*
> \- Martin Luther King

> *Insanity: doing the same thing over and over again*
> *and expecting different results.*
> \- Albert Einstein

Focus Your Attention and Intention

I have chosen to live a life filled with

_____!

The use of Magic demands that you are _____

with yourself. The use of Magic demands your

_____.

And it demands your _____.

If you're going to create the life of your dreams, you must plan for, prepare for, and prize the outcome.

Dream big or go home!

I WANT MORE _____.

Big results require big ambitions.
- Heraclitus

What's the monster that's keeping you from your MORE? Give it a

name._____

If I could be, do, and have anything I need to destroy what's keeping me from having what I want, what would it be, what would I do, or what would I have?

Create Your Magical Mantra

*Every act you have ever performed since the day you were born
was performed because you wanted something.*
- Andrew Carnegie

I Can _____

I Will _____

I Dare _____

I Am _____

Your Magical Toolkit

• What is your Object of Affection and what does it mean to you?

• What are your 10-12 power songs?

Until We Meet Again

Between now and the next Action Group meeting, deeply consider the following questions.

- What do I expect an ecstatic life to be like?

- What am I willing to give in return for living a life of my dreams?

SESSION ONE
THE MAGIC I WANT TO CREATE
(a page for notes that will change my life)

⌘

SESSION ONE
THE MAGIC I WANT TO HELP OTHERS CREATE
(a page for notes that will help me help the others in the group)

⌘

SESSION TWO
I WILL REGAIN MY POWER

The Magic That's Already Started

It probably didn't take long for you to get a sense of the new dynamic that your Action Group has created. You are now _____ on each other—not in a subservient sense, but in a mutually advantageous way.

- How can you help the others in your Action Group to succeed?

Necessary Magic

The universe is full of magical things,
patiently waiting for our wits to sharpen.
- Eden Phillpotts

As a group, start working through Session Two. It is designed to coincide with pages 103-105 of *The Most Magical Secret.* The session leader should use the Answer Key on page 77 to help guide the meeting. When a quote appears, use that to examine how it applies to your choice to be a Magician and your desired outcomes. Take lots of notes in this Action

Guide. Then, have a spirited group discussion and refer back to both your notes and this Action Guide to keep all of you focused and moving forward.

*The only way to predict the future is to have
power to shape the future.*
- Eric Hoffer

*It is folly for a man to pray to the gods for that
which he has the power to obtain himself.*
- Epicurus

Focus Your Attention and Intention

*Trust yourself. Create the kind of self
that you will be happy with all your life.
Make the most of yourself by fanning
the tiny, inner sparks of possibility
into flames of achievement.*
- Golda Meir

Days 1 through 7 all challenge you to finally decide on what you want to create, what that result will actually mean to you and everyone else, and force you to believe in yourself.

DAY 1 OF MAGIC

You want your life to be _____ from what it is right now. To make that happen, you must have a target, a goal, and an outcome in mind. There's one outcome or result—more than anything else—that would change your life in a powerful, profound, and positive way right now.

The one thing I want to manifest more than anything else in the world is

_____

DAY 2 OF MAGIC

_____ always happens. But, you're creating change with a purpose in mind—to feel better and to have more freedom, at the very least. Whatever you're intent on manifesting, there's a change that you have in mind. There's a better life that you're running to meet.

When I achieve my goal, this is how my life will be different:

_____

DAY 3 OF MAGIC

Magicians _____ reality. There are consequences to such a shift. You don't operate in a vacuum. Have you considered what your desired outcome means for everyone else?

When I achieve my goal, this is how I will change the world:

_____

DAY 4 OF MAGIC

Nothing is _____. Certainly not Magic. One of the most rewarding things you can do is determine, in advance, what you're willing to give back to the world in order to get the result you desire. Of course, if you're really going to be "living the dream," you should consider giving back first. You'll be amazed at what happens when you do.

I'm willing to give back to the world by

_____

DAY 5 OF MAGIC

Magicians love a _____. We thrive on finding a wall that most others would look at and say, "Now what? I'm stuck," and then walking through it (or appearing to walk through it). We also flourish when we're told that we can't do something. Those are the situations that truly define us.

People keep telling me that

_____

is impossible. I thrive on challenging the impossible.

DAY 6 OF MAGIC

There are certain things that you take as _____; beliefs that guide your choices and in which you place your confidence. Today, I'm interested in the core belief or beliefs—not general impressions or vague feelings—you must have in order for you to manifest the dreams you have.

I must believe

_____

for my dreams to come true.

DAY 7 OF MAGIC

Remember Einstein's definition of "insanity"? Well, let's get real with each other. There are certain things that you do that simply don't serve your vision of the future well. Stop _____ failure. You can do that by identifying it right now.

I must stop doing

_____

for my dreams to come true.

Your Return to Magic

- What have you discovered about yourself as you chose what you want to create and the results you want to manifest?

- What are you ignoring about your belief system that could still use your attention?

Until We Meet Again

Between now and the next Action Group meeting, deeply consider the following questions.

- What pain is the world experiencing right now that your Magic can fix?

- Assume your friends are all plotting behind your back to make sure you succeed with what you want most in life. What are they saying to each other?

SESSION TWO
THE MAGIC I WANT TO CREATE
(a page for notes that will change my life)

⌘

SESSION TWO
THE MAGIC I WANT TO HELP OTHERS CREATE
(a page for notes that will help me help the others in the group)

⌘

SESSION THREE
I WILL STOP PRETENDING
AND GET ON WITH LIVING

The Difference A Little Focus Makes

For the last 7 days, you've been centered on creating a life of Magic. This new focus should have absorbed you and plunged you into a new appreciation of what your life can be like. You'll also have likely started noticing a _____ of your senses and your observation of all the opportunities available to you.

- What have you discovered about your ability to envision the life you want to live as compared with the life you've been living?

Necessary Magic

Your pain is the breaking of the shell
That encloses your understanding.
- Khalil Gibran

As a group, start working through Session Three. It is designed to coincide with pages 105-106 of *The Most Magical Secret*. The session leader should use the Answer Key on pages 77-78 to help guide the meeting. When a quote appears, use that to examine how it applies to your choice to be a Magician and your desired outcomes. Take lots of notes in this Action Guide. Then, have a spirited group discussion and refer back to both your notes and this Action Guide to keep all of you focused and moving forward.

The more one does and sees and feels,
the more one is able to do, and the more
genuine may be one's appreciation of
fundamental things like home, and love,
and understanding companionship.
- Amelia Earhart

The art of being wise is the art of
knowing what to overlook.
- William James

Focus Your Attention and Intention

Give a small boy a hammer, and he will
find that everything he encounters needs pounding.
- Abraham Kaplan

Days 8 through 14 direct you outside yourself. They force you to start seeing the bigger picture and how everything you say and everything you do (everything you project outward) is intertwined with what you hear and see (everything that is projected at you).

DAY 8 OF MAGIC

Your consistent and replicable success and happiness aren't just about you. They're about those around you, as well. They need you to be successful and happy. Perhaps even more than you need it for yourself. Have you ever considered the possibility that you have an _____ to be prosperous and joyful?

The world needs my dreams to come true as much as me because

_____

DAY 9 OF MAGIC

There is a _____ that lives within you; a truth that keeps you going and fuels your forward motion. That truth might reveal itself to you with messages from the outside. It might make itself known at night while you're sleeping. However it lets you know that it's there, that truth needs to have words put to it so that it becomes even more tangible.

This is how I know I still believe in my dreams

_____

DAY 10 OF MAGIC

Most of us go through life _____ to the strategies of others. It's time for you to carefully consider what has to happen in order for you to have success and happiness. You don't have to determine every little thing that has to happen. But you do have to come up with a game plan of some sort (a road map, if you will) so that you'll know when you're on and off course.

My simple game plan to manifest my dreams is:

_____

DAY 11 OF MAGIC

The world wants you to _____. It wants you to be happy. So much so, in fact, that it always acts in unison with your true desires and needs.

Most of the time it accomplishes all this quietly, privately, and secretly. That is, of course, until you pay attention to it.

The world is conspiring to make my dreams come true by

_____

DAY 12 OF MAGIC

It's so easy to be hard on _____. Perhaps it's time to start being good to yourself, instead. There are things you do that are admirable, responsible, honorable, and in line with your dreams. Let's praise that.

This is what I do correctly:

_____

DAY 13 OF MAGIC

Pain. Danger. Anxiety. These are just some of the things that scare us. It's time to understand that most of our fears are _____. That means we can reprogram and rewire ourselves to enjoy life more and thus earn the delight we crave. It begins with defining what a life without fear looks like.

A life without fear is

_____

DAY 14 OF MAGIC

Each of us needs positive confirmation and optimistic feedback at various times. The fun thing you're going to learn is that the outside world is constantly giving you such messages. You just have to _____. You just have to know what to look for and listen to. You just have figure out, ahead of time, what will (and will not) validate your dream life.

When _____ happens,

I will know I'm on the right track.

Making Magic Real

- Who are you to want dreams so big, and visions so grand, and desires so vivid?

- What do you now know about the relationship between the life you want to live and what the world wants for you?

Until We Meet Again

Between now and the next Action Group meeting, deeply consider the following questions:

- What thoughts are currently consuming you most of the time?

- Where do you want to be in 5 years?

SESSION THREE
THE MAGIC I WANT TO CREATE
(a page for notes that will change my life)

⌘

SESSION THREE
THE MAGIC I WANT TO HELP OTHERS CREATE
(a page for notes that will help me help the others in the group)

⌘

SESSION FOUR
I WILL FIND A WAY FORWARD
AND FOLLOW IT

Magicians Create Important Outcomes

For the last 7 days, you've been pushed beyond your own self. You've experienced the synchronicity that is ever-present in the world. You're also starting to discover that you are always _____ . . . so you must be careful and mindful of what it is you're thinking about.

- What have you discovered about the thoughts, dreams, and desires you hold and how those create the outcomes you experience?

Necessary Magic

Only put off until tomorrow what you are
willing to die having left undone.
- Pablo Picaso

As a group, start working through Session Four. It is designed to coincide with page 106 of *The Most Magical Secret*. The session leader should use the Answer Key on page 78 to help guide the meeting. When a quote appears, use that to examine how it applies to your choice to be a Magician and your desired outcomes. Take lots of notes in this Action Guide. Then, have a spirited group discussion and refer back to both your notes and this Action Guide to keep all of you focused and moving forward.

Success is liking yourself,
liking what you do,
and liking how you do it.
- Maya Angelou

The successful warrior is the average man,
with laser-like focus.
- Bruce Lee

Focus Your Attention and Intention

A gift consists not in what is done or given,
but in the intention of the giver or doer.
- Lucius Annaeus Seneca

Days 15 through 21 are all about motivation. There are reasons that you do what you do, think what you think, and feel what you feel. Let's discover what brings purpose to your life of Magic and what provides you with direction as you move forward towards your goals.

DAY 15 OF MAGIC

When we _____, we send messages to ourselves that confirm we are internally stable, inherently reliable, and fundamentally trustworthy. You are a genuine Magician. Let's stay on track.

I must _____

to continue to be authentic.

DAY 16 OF MAGIC

All great Magic starts with a _____. All great visions begin with a desire. All great desires are born from wanting something different than what we have right now. Imagine what your life will be like 5 years after your dreams come true and that you can have anything you want.

This is what my life will be like 5 years after my dreams come true:

_____

DAY 17 OF MAGIC

You are not a life with a _____. You are a _____ with a life. When you intend to use your Magic to change the world in positive, profound, and powerful ways, it will consume you. It will create a hunger in you such that you can't wait to devour the world and spit it back out as a better place.

Do I think about my Magic 100% of the time? _____

If not, why not?

_____

DAY 18 OF MAGIC

A dream without _____ is feeble and impotent. A dream without doing is like thinking about a marvelous meal and never actually tasting the food. Yes, every step you take in the direction of your dreams brings you that much closer to the manifestation of what you want. Still, there is that one BIG step you can take. That risk. That exhilarating action you can engage in that you know, deep in your heart and soul, has to happen for your desired outcome to materialize.

The biggest step I could take to make my dreams come true is

_____

DAY 19 OF MAGIC

Once   you   choose   a   life   of   Magic,   everything
_____. You. Your friends. Your family. The
world. Life becomes brighter. People become allies. Time flows in your
direction. You get everything you need. What if you walked away from all
that?

If I had to give up my dreams, this is what would happen to me:

_____

DAY 20 OF MAGIC

"Grand." "Earthshaking." "Meaningful." "Big." Use whatever word you
want,   there's   something   you   need   to   do   before   you
_____. Some people refer to it as a "Calling."
Others might call it a restlessness to make a dent in the Universe. The
title doesn't matter. That you recognize it does.

_____

is my important work.

DAY 21 OF MAGIC

Most people have _____ feelings - those little
tickles in their imagination that signal something is going to happen (and
for them, it's usually some imagined bad event). Consistently successful
Magicians have expectations, as well, but their expectations are of
outcomes waiting to happen. That also implies, of course, that certain
outcomes aren't going to happen.

I don't expect

_____

to happen today.

Making Magic Real

• How do you define "intention"?

• What is the most meaningful thing that has happened to you since you chose to live a life of Magic?

Until We Meet Again

Between now and the next Action Group meeting, deeply consider the following questions:

• If you could experience any feeling at all on a moment's notice, what would you choose?

• Why is it important for you to take a stand for what you believe in?

SESSION FOUR
THE MAGIC I WANT TO CREATE
(a page for notes that will change my life)

⌘

SESSION FOUR
THE MAGIC I WANT TO HELP OTHERS CREATE
(a page for notes that will help me help the others in the group)

⌘

SESSION FIVE
I WILL OPEN THE SECRET DOOR
TO A REAL LIFE

Magic Lets Us Feel Better

So many times, we let our _____ happen to us and dictate what will happen throughout the day rather than choosing how we are going to feel and how we are going to direct our feelings to serve us well. I am not suggesting that you deny a particular feeling (sometimes you just wake up in "one of those moods"). And I'm not suggesting that you battle against how you're "feeling." I am recommending, when you have an uncomfortable or unwanted feeling, that you recognize it, seek the real message that it's sending to you (and it might involve some digging), and only then choose a more empowering emotion. You really do have that option.

- What is the difference between reacting and responding to situations, feelings, things, and people?

Necessary Magic

Life isn't about finding yourself.
Life is about creating yourself.
- George Bernard Shaw

As a group, start working through Session Five. It is designed to coincide with page 106 of *The Most Magical Secret*. The session leader should use the Answer Key on page 78 to help guide the meeting. When a quote appears, use that to examine how it applies to your choice to be a Magician and your desired outcomes. Take lots of notes in this Action Guide. Then, have a spirited group discussion and refer back to both your notes and this Action Guide to keep all of you focused and moving forward.

> *The highest manifestation of life consists in this:*
> *that a being governs its own actions.*
> *A thing which is always subject to the direction of another*
> *is somewhat of a dead thing.*
> - Thomas Aquinas

> *Success depends on previous preparation, and*
> *without such preparation there is sure to be failure.*
> - Confucius

> *If you don't stand for something,*
> *you'll fall for anything.*
> - Alexander Hamilton

Focus Your Attention and Intention

> *You can't depend on your eyes when*
> *your imagination is out of focus.*
> - Mark Twain

Days 22 through 28 are all about choosing what your Magic means (to yourself and others). That also entails finally deciding what you don't want your Magic to mean. It is up to you, as a Magician, to manage any given situation. If you can't manage the situation, then you can at least manage how you respond to it. Consistently successful Magicians have learned that in order to achieve their goals they must remain observant and attentive for things and people who might stand in the way of those goals.

DAY 22 OF MAGIC

Have you ever noticed that most of the time you get just what you've been _____ for? That, if you wake up in a bad mood, the day just goes badly? That, if you wake up in an ecstatic mood, the very same day is just spectacular? I want you to get used to waking up each morning and crafting a powerful, positive, and profound "feeling" that something wonderful is going to happen to you.

I expect

_____

to happen today.

DAY 23 OF MAGIC

If I was to ask your closest friend what you represent or symbolize, what would they say? What would your most intimate partner say? What would your nemesis say? Powerful Magicians are _____ of something. There doesn't have to be anything arbitrary about it, by the way. Make a choice—right here and right now—of the significance you want to impart.

I stand for

_____

DAY 24 OF MAGIC

I write a lot about the power of choice and giving yourself permission to be, do, and have anything you desire. That means saying "yes" to yourself and others and opportunity a lot of the time. But, there comes a time when you have to say "_____." And you have to understand what the boundary is that you won't tolerate being crossed in order to have an effective "no." So, what do you "no"?

I stand against

_____

DAY 25 OF MAGIC

Okay, we've talked about grand dreams and impressive desires and heroic outcomes. Those are certainly wielded by great Magicians with staggering effectiveness. There's also a time to just focus on the _____ future; the baby steps that need to be taken before you run. You know the ones—the small sequences you put into play and the small steps you take that, when viewed together, create the life path you have chosen.

My journey of a thousand steps begins today with

_____

DAY 26 OF MAGIC

How is your Magic _____ by others? More importantly, how do you want your Magic perceived by others? Those two things are not necessarily the same. It's time to carefully examine the impression you actually leave on others. This is not an exercise in choosing "how" you want your Magic noticed. This is an exercise in you getting real with what is actually happening to those around you. You won't change something if you don't know there's a problem. And you won't keep doing what's working if you don't recognize the successes.

My Magic makes others feel

_____

DAY 27 OF MAGIC

You've chosen a life of Magic because of how it makes you _____ on physical, mental, and emotional levels. I want you to have confidence that you've made the right decision. I want you to come to know why you've chosen this type of life because once you move beyond vague impressions about a life of Magic and get to a place of deep understanding, there will be no stopping you!

My Magic makes me feel

_____

DAY 28 OF MAGIC

There's one "_____" (and I'm using that term very loosely here so don't confine yourself—I haven't) that makes you feel treasured, adored, complete, and safe. Oh, there are lots of things that can combine for that type of feeling. You might even feel compelled on first blush to name a person because you feel that to answer otherwise would make you unfaithful. Let's move past all that, though, and get right down to it. I want you to discover where your life force actually comes from.

---

makes me feel loved.
(Hint: Don't just answer with "My Magic.")

Making Magic Real

- What additional decisions do you know you need to make in order to have an ecstatic life?

- Who is already living a life or has achievements you'd like to emulate? If you could ask that person one question about success and happiness, what would it be? What do you imagine they would answer?

Until We Meet Again

Between now and the next Action Group meeting, deeply consider the following questions:

- What do you want your magical legacy to be?

- What do you have to continue to think, feel, do, and be in order for your Magic to have even more impact on yourself and others?

SESSION FIVE
THE MAGIC I WANT TO CREATE
(a page for notes that will change my life)

⌘

SESSION FIVE
THE MAGIC I WANT TO HELP OTHERS CREATE
(a page for notes that will help me help the others in the group)

⌘

SESSION SIX
I WILL LIVE A LIFE
THAT TRULY MATTERS

Create a Legacy of Magic

- Just like you did at the beginning of your first gathering, go around the room and get to know each other all over again. Introduce yourself as if no one knew you.

- How do you describe Magic now compared with how you described it when your first gathered? What's different about you? What's different about your Magic? What's different about your confidence, attitude, and abilities?

Your decisions, your actions, and your outcomes all help _____ you. In the 28 Days of Magic that you have just completed, you have discovered what really matters to you. You have made breakthroughs that have forged a new you and you have uncovered things you used to do and thoughts you used to think that are of no use anymore. Throughout your journey you have had incredible insights. During your Action Group meetings you have taken exciting and clear notes. Now is the time to take all that you've learned and understand the truth that is there for you. You made a promise to yourself early on. Now is the time to bring that promise and your truth boldly together so that you start living a life that truly matters.

- Now that you can be, do, and have everything you want, what do you dream about?

Necessary Magic

Imagination rules the world.
- Napoleon Bonaparte

As a group, start working through Session Six. It is designed to coincide with pages 112-129 of *The Most Magical Secret*. The session leader should use the Answer Key on page 79 to help guide the meeting. When a quote appears, use that to examine how it applies to your choice to be a Magician and your desired outcomes. Take lots of notes in this Action Guide. Then, have a spirited group discussion and refer back to both your notes and this Action Guide to keep all of you focused and moving forward.

To be nobody but yourself in a world
which is doing its best,
night and day, to make you everybody else
means to fight the hardest battle
which any human being can fight;
and never stop fighting.
- e.e. cummings

I, not events, have the power
to make me happy or unhappy today.
I can choose which it shall be.
Yesterday is dead,
tomorrow hasn't arrived yet.
I have just one day, today,
and I'm going to be happy in it.
- Groucho Marx

All of them had a restlessness in common.
- John Steinbeck, *East of Eden*

Focus Your Attention and Intention

The soul should always stand ajar,
ready to welcome the ecstatic experience.
- Emily Dickinson

I've been pretty bold in telling you that you can live an
_____ life. I've also been pretty honest in *The Most Magical Secret* in admitting that shit happens . . . even to Magicians. While living a life of Magic can certainly be a solitary practice, I assure you that sharing your Magic with others is the most satisfying of all. It keeps you real. It keeps you focused. It provides you with a safety net (or in some cases pushes you out of the nest so you can fly). The group you have been meeting with is one type of support system. You have many other options. Take the time to consider how you can share your new life with others because there are countless others just waiting to see how you've made all this work. They want the same type of life. And you are now a shining example for them.

Every solution brings new _____.

Every outcome brings new _____.

Every creation brings an _____ to something else.

- Discuss amongst yourselves the new challenges you face.

- Discuss amongst yourselves the new desires you feel.

- Create an impromptu ceremony for bidding farewell to your old way of living and for blessing that which you have put behind you.

- Create an impromptu ceremony honoring your life as a Magician.

Making Magic Real

- What is your plan for taking your Magic to an even deeper level?

- Who else do you plan on talking to about all this? Who do you believe can really benefit from learning about their own Magic?

- Create a sanctuary—real or imaginary—where you can go to be at one with yourself, get your thoughts in order, and plan for your Magic!

Until We Meet Again

This particular Action Group sequence might have ended, but that doesn't mean your group has to. If you were to take your Action Group to the next level of effectiveness, what would have to happen?

•　　　How can your new family of Magicians combine their skills and abilities to make the world a better place?

•　　　If you were writing an Action Guide for the next incarnation of your group, what would you say?

SESSION SIX
THE MAGIC I WANT TO CREATE
(a page for notes that will change my life)

⌘

SESSION SIX
THE MAGIC I WANT TO HELP OTHERS CREATE
(a page for notes that will help me help the others in the group)

⌘

FREQUENTLY ASKED QUESTIONS

How long is this Action Group going to last?

This Action Guide is designed to cover a 6-week period. During that 6 weeks, you will have 1 week of preparation followed by your 28 Days of Magic (divided over 4 sessions) and then ending with 1 closing session. You always have the option to form a new group at the conclusion of the 6-week period. I think it would be wonderful, of course, if your initial group continues to meet, perhaps grows, and takes the lessons to an even more intense and significant level.

I want you excited to belong to this select group of people. You should be honored that you were asked to participate. Still, bear in mind that you have pledged to be part of a magical family of sorts. That means you will be highly focused and intensely committed to your group for 6 weeks. It's optional if you want to continue onward with the group after that. But, during the 6 weeks, please be duty-bound in your sharing with the others, your honoring of what you hear and see, and your presence.

What if I don't like how the group is being led?

We're all human (although some of you won't want to admit that out loud). We have our idiosyncrasies. More importantly, this is a group of Magicians. That means you're all likely A-type personalities and you know what happens when you get a room full of "those types." I recommend that you carefully consider all of this when you ponder joining the others in the first place. I have a feeling, however, that the mere fact that you've been asked to be part of this inner gathering is enough to guarantee all of you are ultimately a good fit for each other. You have the book and this Action Guide. Those are the things to which you will ultimately adhere. Your host is a guide, a supporter, and wants nothing more than for all of you to succeed. Let them do that! John Lennon once said, "Everything will be okay in the end. If it's not okay, it's not the end."

What happens if we want to add new members sometime after the first session and during the following 5 weeks?

This is going to be your biggest challenge because adding new members certainly adds more vitality and freshness to your Action Group. At the same time, the original members are all moving forward with the various sessions and the new member might not be caught up to you for a variety of reasons. While the excitement of adding a new member might be compelling, I recommend that you let a prospective member attend one meeting to "see what it's like" with the understanding that they will be part of the "next" group. In this fashion, you can start readying for either an expanded Action Group or for a new Action Group (whichever you prefer).

If you do decide to add new members in the midst of your 6 weeks of sessions, please don't rush anyone to "catch up." They need the time and nurturing and experience to create and use their own Magic. This means you might have to carve out some additional time during your sessions to essentially back-track for the original members over ground that has already been covered. The really fascinating thing about doing this, by the way, is that each of the original members will no doubt discover things and thoughts and additional feelings they either glossed over the first time or weren't aware of when they initially did their magical work.

Where do we meet?

You have many, many options. You can meet in someone's home. You can rotate to various members' homes. You can gather at a restaurant. You can get together at someone's office boardroom or conference room. Depending on the time of day, you could assemble at a park or other natural locale.

Well, let's start with the fact that many, if not all, of these sessions will run 1 ½ - 2 hours depending on your group size and the length of the discussion. That's going to eliminate some locations. For example, I don't recommend taking over restaurant space for that long without first letting a manager know that you are having a "business meeting" and it could be lengthy. I've been very candid with managers about the need for space and privacy and have had some who've given my group a secluded area to camp out in. Of course, we order food, beverages, dessert, and leave a very nice tip. Remember, restaurants need to turn tables and wait staff need to make a living.

If you're going to meet in someone's home, be respectful and treat it as if it was your own home. Better yet, treat it as if it isn't your home. Leave it better than you found it. Your sessions are not meant to be onerous or an imposition on any individual or their family. This is all about having fun, finding yourself, and sharing your dreams (and Magic) with others.

Some groups will have members spread out over a large area. If you are still looking for places to consider for your meetings, take a look at some of the websites that cater to just such a situation like:

http://www.meetways.com

http://www.whatshalfway.com

http://www.geomidpoint.com/meet

Can we meet through video chat or by phone?

There are many groups that meet through Google Hangouts, Skype, FaceTime, and similar virtual applications and programs. While the use of such technology certainly has its advantages, there is nothing that beats face-to-face time with each other. Moreover, unless you're meeting in a private place, streaming video in a restaurant is usually not practical simply because it's not quiet and it's not private.

I find phone meetings (audio only) even more disempowering.

If you are faced with not meeting at all versus internet streaming or the phone, then, by all means, do what you need to do to keep your sessions going and the momentum building. But, please don't sacrifice the personal touch for the sake of being able to cross great expanses through your computer or smartphone.

Do I get a certificate for completing the 6 weeks of sessions?

No. But you do get a new you. You also get a new outlook about life. You get a new magical family. You certainly get a new disposition. And you get new dreams.

A certificate does not make you magical. Doing Magic makes you magical.

Am I being asked to join an organized religion or sect?

This Action Guide and the recommended sessions were not designed to be subject to nor allied with or against any particular religion or spiritual system of belief. However, there might be particular groups who, out of a commonality of beliefs and experiences, decide to work through these sessions together and in the context of those beliefs and experiences. The organizer of the Action Group should tell you, in advance, if this is the case.

Is there a fee for being in this magical group?

I don't recommend charging any type of fee for being part of this special group. Of course, you can pay for your own meals and beverages or put a pot of money together for family-style nourishment.

MY ACTION GROUP PLEDGE

By now you know that I take your participation in this Action Group and the use of this Action Guide very seriously. As such, I have put together the following personal pledge for you to use as you see fit. May it serve you well!

> I ASK that you listen to my truth, my passions, and my desired outcomes. By giving voice to that truth, those passions, and those outcomes, I am committed to making my Magic a reality.
>
> I BRING each of you my undefended heart. I know that Magic works best when it is shared.
>
> I GIVE freely of my knowledge, integrity, and expertise. I am here to support you, nurture you, keep you responsible for your actions, and motivate you to live your Magic.
>
> I OFFER my passion and commitment to the entire group. We now have a special bond through our Magic.
>
> I ACT to make my Magic real and my dreams come true. Following every gathering, I will review what we have studied and what I have learned and prepare for our next time together.

I EXPECT an atmosphere of cooperation and collaboration. We are here to help uncover, grow, and support each other's Magic.

I TRUST that each of you will help me to complete my 4 Weeks to an ecstatic life.

I CHOOSE a life of Magic. I alone get to decide the positive, profound, and powerful magical outcomes that are right for me.

WHERE TO FIND OTHER MAGICIANS

Napoleon Hill described a mastermind group as:

> *The coordination of knowledge and effort of two or more people,*
> *who work toward a definite purpose, in the spirit of harmony.*

Benjamin Franklin outlined his Junto group like this:

> *I should have mentioned before, that, in the autumn of the preceding year,*
> *I had form'd most of my ingenious acquaintance into*
> *a club of mutual improvement, which we called the Junto;*
> *we met on Friday evenings.*

First and foremost, you want to consider members who you want to be around and with whom you trust sharing. You are not in competition with each other. This isn't a race. Your group is meant to be fun and educational and empowering.

You can draw members from your immediate and extended family, your colleagues at work, people who already belong to some other type of group you are already a part of, your religious or spiritual community, and even the place where you exercise.

Please remember that your magical group is not just about your personal success and happiness. It is also about personal relationships. Consider people you actually "know" rather than those with whom you only have a passing acquaintance. However, there will be those people who enter into your life who you just instantly have an affinity for and who seem to "get" you. There will come a time when you just have to trust your gut on who to invite.

Make a list of three people from each of the following groups you might consider inviting to your Action Group:

IMMEDIATE FAMILY

1. _____

2. _____

3. _____

EXTENDED FAMILY

1. _____

2. _____

3. _____

WORK COLLEAGUES

1. _____

2. _____

3. _____

MEMBERS OF OTHER GROUPS

1. _____
2. _____
3. _____

RELIGIOUS FAMILY

1. _____
2. _____
3. _____

SPIRITUAL FAMILY

1. _____
2. _____
3. _____

FRIENDS

1. _____
2. _____
3. _____

YOUR MAGICAL GROUP CALENDAR

DATE	SESSION	LOCATION	TIME
	1		
	2		
	3		
	4		
	5		
	6		

ANSWER KEY

SESSION ONE

- I have chosen to live a life filled with **MAGIC**!
- The use of Magic demands that you are **TRUTHFUL** with yourself.
- The use of Magic demands your **SINCERITY**.
  And it demands your **CONCENTRATION.**

SESSION TWO

- You are now **DEPENDENT** on each other.
- You want your life to be **DIFFERENT**.
- **CHANGE** always happens.
- Magicians **TRANSFORM** reality.
- Nothing is **FREE**.
- Magicians love a **CHALLENGE**.
- There are certain things that you take as **TRUE** . . .
- Stop **COPYING** failure.

SESSION THREE

- You'll also have likely started noticing a **SHARPENING** of your senses.

- Have you ever considered the possibility that you have an **OBLIGATION** to be prosperous and joyful?
- There is a **TRUTH** that lives within you . . .
- Most of us go through life **REACTING** to the strategies of others.
- The world wants you to **SUCCEED**.
- It's so easy to be hard on **YOURSELF**.
- It's time to understand that most of our fears are **LEARNED**.
- You just have to **PAY ATTENTION**.

SESSION FOUR

- You're also starting to discover that you are always **SUCCESSFUL** . . .
- When we **SAY AND DO**, we send messages to ourselves . . .
- All great Magic starts with a **VISION**.
- You are not a life with a **PURPOSE**. You are a **PURPOSE** with a life.
- A dream without **ACTION** is feeble and impotent.
- Once you choose a life of Magic, everything **CHANGES**.
- . . . there's something you need to do before you **DIE**.
- Most people have **HAPHAZARD** feelings . . .

SESSION FIVE

- So many times, we let our **EMOTIONS** happen to us . . .
- Have you ever noticed that, most of the time, you get just what you've been **LOOKING** for?
- Powerful Magicians are **SYMBOLS** of something.
- But, there comes a time when you have to say "**NO**."
- There's also a time to just focus on the **IMMEDIATE** future . . .
- How is your Magic **PERCEIVED** by others?
- You've chosen a life of Magic because of how it makes you **FEEL** on physical, mental, and emotional levels.
- There's one "**THING**" . . . that makes you feel treasured, adored, complete, and safe.

SESSION SIX

- Your decisions, your actions, and your outcomes all help **DEFINE** you.
- I've been pretty bold in telling you that you can live an **ECSTATIC** life.
- Every solution brings new **CHALLENGES**.
- Every outcome brings new **DESIRES**.
- Every creation brings an **END** to something else.

A NOTE ON THE AUTHOR

Scott Grossberg is hired to make individuals and businesses more positive, more powerful, and more productive. He works with others to take their lives and their dreams of success in incredible new directions. There is a reason why some of the largest and most respected businesses in the world have put their trust in him. Scott's lectures and workshops have directly impacted thousands of people around the world. He is one of the founding partners of the AV-rated, California law firm of Cihigoyenetche, Grossberg & Clouse. Scott is a member of the National Speakers Association, the Academy of Magical Arts (the Magic Castle in Hollywood), the International Brotherhood of Magicians, the Psychic Entertainers Association, and the British Society of Mystery Performers. He lives in Southern California.

scottgrossberg.com
scottgrossberg.wordpress.com
facebook.com/scottgrossberg
@sgrossberg

MORE OF THE MAGIC I WANT TO CREATE
(a page for more notes that will change my life)

⌘

MORE OF THE MAGIC I WANT TO CREATE

(a page for more notes that will change my life)

⌘

MORE OF THE MAGIC I WANT TO CREATE
(a final page for the notes that will change my life)

⌘

www.ingramcontent.com/pod-product-compliance
Lightning Source LLC
Chambersburg PA
CBHW031538040426
42445CB00010B/602